Animal Neighbours

Owl

D1434809

Stephen Savage

WAYLAND

Animal Neighbours

Titles in this series:

Badger • Bat • Blackbird • Deer • Duck • Fox • Hare • Hedgehog
Mole • Mouse • Otter • Owl • Rat • Snake • Swallow • Toad

Conceived and produced for Hodder Wayland by

Nutshell
MEDIA

Intergen House, 65–67 Western Road, Hove BN3 2JQ, UK
www.nutshellmedialtd.co.uk

Commissioning Editor: Vicky Brooker
Designer: Tim Mayer
Illustrator: Jackie Harland
Picture Research: Glass Onion Pictures

Published in Great Britain in 2004 by Hodder Wayland, an imprint of Hodder Children's Books.
This paperback edition published in 2006.
Reprinted in 2007 and 2009 by Wayland, a division of Hachette Children's Books.
© Copyright 2004 Wayland

British Library Cataloguing in Publication Data
Savage, Stephen, 1965–
Owl. – (Animal neighbours)
1. Owls – Juvenile literature
I. Title
598.9'7

ISBN 978 0 7502 4853 2

Cover: A young tawny owl perched on a tree stump.
Title page: A tawny owl looks out from its nest in the hole of a tree trunk.

Picture acknowledgements
FLPA 7 (Ron Austing), 8 (M. Callan), 10 (Mike Jones), 11 (Roger Hosking), 15, 20 (J. Hawkins), 21
(D. T. Grewcock), 26 (Alan Parker), 27 (David Hosking), 28t (Mike Jones); naturepl.com 6 (Pete Oxford),
9 (Artur Tabor), 13 (Bengt Lundberg), 28b (Bengt Lundberg); NHPA *Title page* (Manfred Danegger), 12,
16 (Melvin Gray), 17 (Manfred Danegger), 19 (Melvin Gray), 22 (Ernie James), 23 (Melvin Gray),
24 (Manfred Danegger), 25 (Michael Leach), 28r (Melvin Gray), 28l (Ernie James);
rspb-images.com *Cover* (Mark Hamblin), 14 (Bill Paton).

Printed and bound in China.

Hachette Children's Books
338 Euston Road, London NW1 3BH

Wayland is a division of Hachette Children's Books, an Hachette UK Company.
www.hachette.co.uk

Contents

Meet the Owl

The owl is a nocturnal bird of prey. There are 167 species of owl alive today. They live in woodlands, forests, grasslands, deserts, and even in cities.

This book is about the tawny owl, a medium-sized owl that is found across Europe and north-west Asia.

◀ The red shading on this map shows where tawny owls live in the world today.

OWL FACTS

The tawny owl was named after the colour of its feathers – 'tawny' meaning 'golden brown'. Its scientific name is *Strix aluco*.

Tawny owls have an average body length of 38 cm and a wingspan of 95–105 cm.

Males weigh an average of 400 g and females weigh up to 590 g.

The tawny owl is the largest type of owl in Britain. In Europe, the European eagle owl is bigger.

Eyes

The owl's eyes are large and provide good night vision. They are positioned on the front of the head, which is good for judging the distance of prey.

Facial disc

The owl's facial disc is an arrangement of small, stiff feathers that form the owl's face. It helps the owl's hearing by collecting sound waves and deflecting them to its ears.

Body

The owl's body is covered with feathers that are a golden brown above and paler underneath. The feathers are patterned with darker bands of brown. They provide both warmth and camouflage.

Legs

The legs are short and covered with feathers.

▲ This shows the size of a tawny owl compared to a domestic cat.

4

Ears

The owl's ears are internal and hidden beneath the edge of the facial disc. One ear is slightly higher than the other, which helps to pinpoint the direction of sound with great accuracy.

Beak

The beak is small but very sharp.

Neck

Unlike our necks, which have seven bones, an owl's neck contains 14 bones. They allow the owl to turn its head right around to see behind it.

Wings

The rounded wings are covered with soft feathers, which allow the owl to fly silently and take its prey by surprise.

Feet

The feet are large and strong for grasping prey. Each of the four toes ends in a razor-sharp talon.

◀ **The tawny owl.**

The Owl Family

▲ A pel's fishing owl carries its catch to the shore in its talons and tears it into smaller pieces using its beak.

Owls belong to a group of birds called raptors, which also includes eagles and hawks. All raptors are birds of prey, with large eyes, sharp beaks and hooked talons. They hunt and eat mainly small mammals and birds.

Most owls are nocturnal, but some species are active during the daytime. The fishing owls of Africa and Asia hunt in daylight. Instead of small mammals, they swoop down from branches of trees and snatch fish from rivers, lakes and shallow waters.

Not all owls live in trees. The burrowing owl from the North American grasslands lives in the burrows of other animals, such as gopher tortoises or prairie dogs. If there are no other burrows available, it digs its own burrow. The elf owl of North America makes its home in old woodpecker nest holes made in giant Saguaro cacti.

BIGGEST AND SMALLEST

The largest owl is the great grey owl of Canada and Alaska, which can grow up to 84 cm long.

The smallest owls are the elf owl of south-western USA and western Mexico, and the least pygmy owl of Brazil, which both grow to about 13 cm long.

► Elf owls often shelter in a hole inside a cactus plant during the heat of the day and hunt at night when it is cooler.

7

Birth and Growing Up

It is spring, and a pregnant female tawny owl prepares her nest, ready to lay her eggs. This might be in a hollow tree, or the abandoned nest of another bird. Over the next few days the female owl lays up to four eggs, about 48 hours apart.

EGGS AND CHICKS

Tawny owl eggs are round and white. A group of eggs is called a clutch.

New-born owls are called chicks. Young owls are called owlets. A group of owlets born at the same time is called a brood.

As soon as each egg is laid, the female carefully sits on it. She uses the brood patch on her belly to keep the eggs warm and safe, while the chicks grow inside. The brood patch has fewer feathers, which allows the mother's warm body to heat the eggs.

▼ A female tawny owl incubates her eggs in a barn to keep them warm.

▲ This chick is the first of the clutch to hatch. Owl chicks have an egg tooth at the tip of their beaks, which they use to break out of the tough eggshell. This drops off a week or two after hatching.

The owl will incubate her eggs in this way for about 28 days, until they are ready to hatch. She only leaves the nest for a short time to defecate or to stretch her wings. Meanwhile, the male does all the hunting and brings her food. During the day, the female sleeps in the nest while the male sleeps nearby.

After about four weeks, the chicks start to peck their way out of the eggs and immediately collapse, exhausted, on the bottom of the nest. The chicks hatch about two days apart, starting with the first egg that was laid. The chicks are born with their eyes closed and with only a thin coat of downy feathers, so the female continues to keep them warm. The male now has to bring food for the chicks as well.

▲ These young chicks lie beside a pile of dead mice stored there by their parents.

Early days

The male owl continues to bring voles and other small mammals to the nest three or four times a night. The female holds the prey with her talons and uses her sharp, hooked beak to tear it into smaller pieces for the owlets to swallow.

The female starts by feeding the most active owlet first, which is usually the first hatchling. This owlet will grow the fastest, while its brothers and sisters will be smaller. The last owlet to hatch will be the smallest of all.

Once the owlets are 1–2 weeks old they will have a thicker coat of downy feathers. Their mother no longer needs to keep them warm and she may leave the nest to hunt. She never stays away for long, however, and soon returns to the nest or a nearby branch. The male continues to bring food to the female, which she feeds to the owlets.

▼ When their mother returns to the nest with prey, the owlets stand and jostle each other for the food.

Leaving the nest

When the owlets are about 4 weeks old, they are able to swallow a whole vole or mouse caught by their parents. They now look like scruffy versions of adult owls and start to leave the cramped nest, climbing up nearby branches.

During the daytime, the owlets huddle together on a branch near the nest for comfort and warmth. At night, the parent owls bring food back to the owlets, finding them by following their hissing squawks.

▲ Owls occasionally catch young rabbits, which make a large meal for their young.

FALLING OUT

When owlets become more active they sometimes fall out of the nest. They can pull themselves back up using their claws and their beak. Their parents will keep feeding the owlets and allow them to climb back up by themselves. In most cases, owlets that are found on the ground do not need to be rescued by people because they have not been abandoned.

▼ As the owlets grow, their downy white feathers are slowly replaced by golden-brown feathers with darker stripes.

As the weeks pass, the owlets wander further from the nest and start to make their first flights. They start with short distances at first, flying from one branch to another. As they get older, the owlets fly longer distances and start to hunt for their own food. Soon each owlet can eat up to four voles or mice a night. When they are 4 months old, any owlets still in the parents' territory will be chased away. It is time for the young owls to find territories of their own.

Habitat

The owl's favourite habitat is woodland. However, tawny owls are very adaptable and can also be found in city gardens and parks. They will live anywhere that has plenty of prey, as well as trees or overgrown areas in which to rest and sleep.

MOBBING

After a night spent hunting, tawny owls roost on tree branches during the day. Sometimes they are discovered and woken from their sleep by small birds, who see the owl as a threat. The birds will mob the owl by dive-bombing it and give warning calls until it flies away.

▼ This tired tawny owl is asleep in its daytime roost.

Tawny owls can be found in many old churchyards, because they often provide good nest and roost sites. Churchyards are often overgrown, so there is plenty of prey to be found. Once a pair of tawny owls has become established in an area, they will rarely travel far. Due to their nocturnal habits, tawny owls are more likely to be heard than seen.

▼ A reflective layer in the tawny owl's eyes helps it to see in this dimly lit churchyard.

Nest and territory

Tawny owls are not good nest-builders. Their favourite nest site is a hollow tree, which will give the best shelter from predators and the weather. They frequently use the abandoned nests of other birds such as crows, and may even use an old squirrel's dray. In areas with a very good food supply but few trees, tawny owls will even nest on the ground. Once they have found a good nest site, a pair of tawny owls may use it year after year.

Tawny owls live with their mate in their own territory. They defend the territory against intruders, including other tawny owls. In late winter and early spring, when many young owls are searching for their own territory, male tawny owls are at their noisiest as they call out defensive warnings.

▲ A female tawny owl guards her four owlets in a nest on the ground.

▶ Nest holes in tree trunks are just large enough for adult owls to enter. This prevents larger predators from entering the nest.

Food and Hunting

Tawny owls hunt at night, so most of their diet is made up of nocturnal animals. They catch and eat a wide variety of prey, both large and small. Their favourite foods are small mammals such as mice, voles, moles and young rabbits. They can also catch bats, either in flight or while they are resting.

▼ Owls are at the top of their food chain. (The illustrations are not to scale.)

Owl food chain

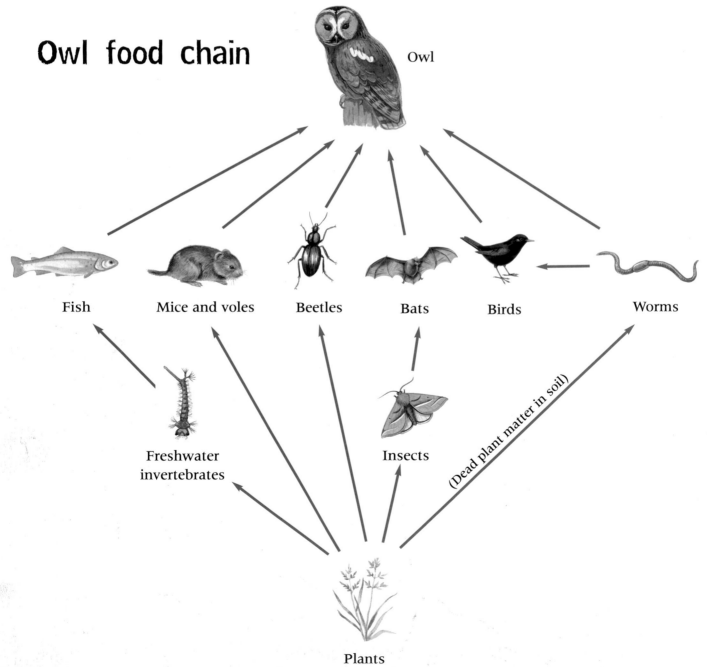

Owl

Fish

Mice and voles

Beetles

Bats

Birds

Worms

Freshwater invertebrates

Insects

(Dead plant matter in soil)

Plants

Tawny owls also eat other birds, especially diurnal (day active) birds as they sleep at night in the branches of trees. In towns and cities, tawny owls prey on blackbirds, sparrows, starlings, blue tits, thrushes and finches. In the countryside, they eat other birds of prey, such as the kestrel and the sparrowhawk.

Other prey in the tawny owl's diet ranges from lizards and frogs to insects and earthworms. Owls may even take fish from parks or garden ponds.

▲ **Earthworms are a good source of moisture and vitamins.**

19

Hunting

The tawny owl's favourite hunting technique is to sit on a tree branch and wait until it spots prey below. Soft fringes on the owl's flight feathers allow it to swoop down on its prey in silence. The prey is usually killed immediately by the owl's powerful feet and talons. Larger prey may be killed with a blow from the owl's beak aimed at the base of its skull.

▼ Small rodents like this mouse make up a large part of a tawny owl's diet.

▲ Conifer trees keep their leaves all year round, so they provide welcome shelter for owls in winter weather.

OWL PELLETS

Owls swallow most animals whole. The skin and soft tissues of their prey are digested, but fur, bones, claws and beaks cannot be digested. The owl regurgitates any undigested parts as a pellet (see page 29), about 12 hours after the prey has been swallowed.

Owls do not hibernate, so the winter can be a very difficult time. Prey is hard to find since small mammals hide away for warmth, or are hidden under a blanket of snow. Out of all the European owls, the adult tawny owl copes the best during severe winters, possibly because it has a more varied diet.

Finding a Mate

Tawny owls become adults between the ages of 1 and 2 years old, when they are ready to find a mate. The male owl produces a courtship 'hooting' call, which is answered by a female. The pair then go through a courtship display before mating. Male and female tawny owls will pair for life. Each year, they go through a similar courtship.

The courtship begins with the male sitting on a branch near the female as he starts to sway from side to side. He then bobs up and down and puffs out his feathers, while making soft grunting sounds. Then the male sidesteps along the branch towards the female and back again. The female may puff out and shake her feathers in response.

▶ A male and female tawny owl are difficult to tell apart because they look very similar.

OWL CALLS

Tawny owls make a variety of calls to communicate with each other. Males call with a hooting 'hooo-hu-hooo' when bringing food to the female in the nest and to warn other males away from their territory. During courtship, males and females call a duet together. After the female calls 'ke-wick', the male replies with a 'hu-hooo', making the owls' most characteristic sound, 'ke-wick hu-hooo'.

In the weeks leading up to mating, the male will offer the female food. They will also spend time preening each other's feathers as a sign of commitment to the task of rearing young.

Tawny owls do not migrate but stay in their territory all year round. This allows them to breed earlier in the year than migratory species of birds.

▲ A male tawny owl will bring the female food to strengthen their bond. The food also gives the female extra energy that is needed to produce her eggs.

Threats

Tawny owls have few natural predators. They usually nest and roost high above the ground and they are quite capable of defending their young against predators. Owls have a long lifespan compared with many other birds. The oldest recorded wild tawny owl was about 19 years old, but in captivity one lived to 27 years old.

▲ The European eagle owl is a powerful predator. It eats rodents, snakes, ducks and smaller owl species such as the tawny owl.

In parts of Europe, tawny owls may be attacked and eaten by the much larger eagle owl, which can reach a length of 75 cm. Owlets that have fallen from the nest may be vulnerable to ground-living mammals such as foxes, cats or dogs. Bad weather can also be disastrous for owlets since their prey hides away for warmth, and as many as half the young owls born may starve to death during a severe winter.

SUPERSTITIONS

Today most people love owls, but it has not always been this way. In the past, some people thought that owls had supernatural abilities because they could see and hunt in the dark. They were associated with witches, and the call of an owl was believed to be a sign that a disaster was about to happen.

▶ This owl is ill and close to starvation, at the end of a long, cold winter.

People and owls

The tawny owl's biggest threat is people. Owls are frequently injured or killed when they fly into the path of vehicles or trains. They also fly into overhead cables that are difficult for them to see.

In the past, gamekeepers shot tawny owls because they killed valuable game birds, such as pheasants and grouse. Thousands of owls were killed and put on display by the gamekeepers, who nailed them to posts.

Tawny owls suffered greatly in the 1950s and 1960s from the widespread use of pesticides on farm crops. The pesticides poisoned the owls' prey. While pesticides are now used more carefully, owls still die by eating rodent pests, such as rats and mice, which have been poisoned.

◀ **Tawny owls are the most common bird of prey to be found dead by the roadside. They can be hit by traffic as they fly low across the road.**

▲ In many countries it is illegal to disturb an owl's nest, whether it is natural or in a nesting box.

NESTING BOXES

Artificial nesting boxes can help tawny owls. The box, which is 75 cm deep with a 20-centimetre square floor is the size of an owl's preferred nest hole. The box has to be placed high up in a tree, in a place that is protected from the sun and the wind.

However, owls have benefited from humans as well. The extensive planting of fast-growing conifer trees for their timber has created lots of nesting sites. Nesting boxes in trees have provided artificial nesting holes in trees that would not normally be suitable. These factors might help to explain why tawny owls are declining slower than most other owl species.

Owl Life Cycle

1 Owl eggs are incubated for 28–30 days. The newly hatched owlets are born with their eyes closed and with only a few downy feathers.

2 By 1 or 2 weeks old, the owlets are covered in a thicker coat of downy feathers and their eyes are open.

3 At 4 weeks old, the owlets start to leave the nest but they are still fed by their parents. They are not yet able to fly.

4 At 4 months old, the young owls leave their parents' territory and set out to find their own.

5 By the age of 1 or 2 years, the owls are ready to breed.

Owl Clues

Look out for the following clues to help you find signs of a owl:

Nest
While owls are difficult to see when they nest in a hollow tree, you may spot one in the entrance to the hole, or in a disused crow's nest or squirrel's dray.

Calls
Owls can be more easily heard than seen. Listen for their calls after dark, particularly their distinctive 'ke-wick hu-hooo'.

Mobbing
If you see or hear lots of small birds dive-bombing a tree during the day, they may be mobbing a sleeping owl.

Feathers
Owls moult their feathers over a period of 2–3 months after they have reared their young. Look out for tawny owl feathers, which are patterned with bands of brown.

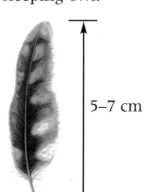

5–7 cm

Owl pellets
Owl pellets can easily be mistaken for droppings, but they are the indigestible remains of an owl's meal, such as bones, fur and feathers. Pellets can be dark grey to brown coloured, furry and with bones visible depending on what the owl has eaten. Pellets may be found beneath a favourite roost site.

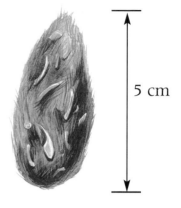

5 cm

Eyeshine
The back layer of an owl's eyes is very reflective. It reflects the light from a torch or car headlights, making the eyes glow at night.

Owlet
Owlets that have temporarily fallen from their tree are sometimes visible on the ground. However, it is dangerous to go near an owlet or an owl's nest because the parents may attack.

Droppings
Like many other birds, owl droppings are small, soft and white. Seen on the ground, they could give away the position of a roosting owl above.

Nature reserves
Wardens sometimes put up owl nesting boxes on nature reserves. There may be one on a reserve near you.

Glossary

bird of prey A bird that eats other animals.

brood A number of chicks produced from one hatching.

camouflage The colour or pattern of some animals that helps them blend in with their surroundings and makes them hard to see.

defecate To get rid of bodily waste, often as a dropping.

digest To break down food into substances that the body can use.

dray The home of a squirrel for resting or rearing young.

habitat The area where an animal or plant naturally lives.

hatch To break out of an egg.

hibernate To enter a deep sleep that lasts most of the winter.

incubate To hatch eggs by sitting on them to keep them warm.

migrate To make a journey between different habitats or countries in particular seasons.

moult To shed feathers before new feathers grow.

nocturnal Sleeping during the day and active at night.

owlets Young owls.

pesticides Chemicals sprayed on crops to kill insect pests.

predator An animal that eats other animals.

prey Animals that are killed and eaten by predators.

regurgitate To throw up. When an owl eats an animal, all the bones, fur and feathers are trapped in a part of the throat called the gizzard. They are regurgitated as a pellet, which the owl ejects from its mouth.

rodent A mammal with sharp teeth used for gnawing. Rats, mice and squirrels are rodents.

roost A place where birds gather to rest or sleep, or the action of resting.

talon The claw of an animal, especially a bird of prey.

territory The area that is defended and controlled by an animal.

Finding Out More

Other books to read

Animal Classification by Polly Goodman (Hodder Wayland, 2004)

Animal Young: Birds by Rod Theodorou (Heinemann, 2000)

Classifying Living Things: Classifying Birds by Andrew Solway (Heinemann, 2004)

From Egg to Adult: The Life Cycle of Birds by Mike Unwin (Heinemann, 2004)

Illustrated Encyclopedia of Animals by Fran Pickering (Chrysalis, 2003)

Junior Nature Guides: Birds by Angela Royston (Chrysalis, 2003)

Life Cycles: Ducks and Other Birds by Sally Morgan (Chrysalis, 2003)

Living Nature: Birds by Angela Royston (Chrysalis, 2005)

The Wayland Book of Common British Birds by Nick Williams (Hodder Wayland, 2000)

What's the Difference?: Birds by Stephen Savage (Hodder Wayland, 2002)

Wild Britain: Towns & Cities, Parks & Gardens, Woodlands by R. & L. Spilsbury (Heinemann, 2003)

Organisations to contact

Countryside Foundation for Education
PO Box 8, Hebden Bridge HX7 5YJ
www.countrysidefoundation.org.uk
An organisation that produces training and teaching materials to help people understand the countryside.

English Nature
Northminster House, Peterborough, Cambridgeshire PE1 1UA
www.englishnature.org.uk
A government body that promotes the conservation of English wildlife and the natural environment.

The Hawk and Owl Trust
PO Box 100, Taunton, TA4 2WX
www.hawkandowl.org
A wild birds of prey conservation group with an education centre and a website containing facts and details of events.

RSPB
www.rspb.org.uk
A wild birds conservation charity with wildlife reserves and a website that includes an A-Z of UK birds, news, surveys and webcams about issues concerning wild birds.

Wildlife Watch
National Office, The Kiln, Waterside, Mather Road, Newark NG24 1WT
www.wildlifetrusts.org
The junior branch of the Wildlife Trusts, a network of local Wildlife Trusts caring for nature reserves, and protecting a huge number of habitats and species.

Index

Page numbers in **bold** refer to a photograph or illustration.